**SIDNEY CENTER
BRANCH LIBRARY**

Anorexia

Rachel Lynette

KIDHAVEN PRESS

An imprint of Thomson Gale, a part of The Thomson Corporation

Detroit • New York • San Francisco • San Diego • New Haven, Conn. • Waterville, Maine • London • Munich

© 2006 Thomson Gale, a part of The Thomson Corporation.

Thomson and Star Logo are trademarks and Gale and KidHaven Press are registered trademarks used herein under license.

For more information, contact
KidHaven Press
27500 Drake Rd.
Farmington Hills, MI 48331-3535
Or you can visit our Internet site at http://www.gale.com

LIBRARY OF CONGRESS CATALOGING-IN-PUBLICATION DATA

Lynette, Rachel.
    Anorexia / by Rachel Lynette.
        p. cm. — (Understanding diseases and disorders)
    Includes bibliographical references and index.
    ISBN 0-7377-3176-1 (hardcover : alk. paper)
    1. Anorexia nervosa—Juvenile literature. I. Title. II. Series.
    RC552.A5L97 2005
    616.85'262—dc22

                                                        2005007806

Printed in the United States of America

Contents

Chapter One

What Is Anorexia?

Anorexia nervosa, better known simply as anorexia, is a serious eating disorder. Although it is an emotional disorder, anorexia can cause permanent physical damage and sometimes even death. People who develop anorexia usually start off by dieting to lose weight. But rather than choosing a healthy diet that includes a wide variety of food from all of the food groups, people who have anorexia starve themselves. They eat only small amounts of just a few low-calorie foods. These foods do not provide enough calories or nutrients to maintain a healthy body. Anorexics lose weight rapidly and then continue to starve themselves, even when they are very thin.

Allie talks about how anorexia has affected her life:

It all began as skipping one meal after being called a "fat pig." It escalated from there. I was skipping two meals a day and eating just an apple and three saltine crackers for dinner. I lost weight rapidly and caught the attention of my family doctor. I was afraid to eat and was hospitalized because I refused to eat and continued to lose weight, despite the threats of my family to force-feed me. I was hospitalized for a total of four times within an eight

People who develop anorexia live in constant fear of gaining weight and only eat small amounts of low-calorie foods.

month period. Today, I am still anorexic, but I'm in therapy and see a nutritionist. I'm slowly recovering from the disease that nearly ruined my family and ruined my life.[1]

The word *anorexia* means "loss of appetite"; however, anorexics do not lose their appetites. In fact, because they eat so little, anorexics are constantly

Anorexics step on the scale several times each day to make sure their weight stays low.

hungry. An anorexic's life is almost entirely focused on food and weight. Anorexics spend a lot of time thinking about food. An anorexic might cook elaborate meals for others or collect recipes and watch cooking shows on TV. Most anorexics know a great deal about the calories, fat, and carbohydrates that different foods contain. They use this knowledge to stay thin rather than for healthy eating.

When Christy developed anorexia, she became obsessed with calories. In her diary she wrote, "I want to learn the caloric content in everything. I wonder how many calories are in a postage stamp. Do vitamins have calories? I know a stick of gum has 10 calories, but if I were to chew gum instead of eating lunch, I'd come out way ahead."[2]

Anorexics **obsess** about the food they eat, analyzing how many calories they consume. They have intense feelings of guilt if they feel they have eaten too much. They may also spend a lot of time thinking about their weight and may weigh themselves frequently. Kim, a recovered anorexic, says, "I constantly stood on the scale to see what the number was and it always determined how my day would go—whether or not I could eat."[3]

Too Thin

People who maintain a weight 15 percent below the lowest weight recommended for their age and height are considered anorexic. A thirteen-year-old girl who is 5 feet, 4 inches tall (163cm) should weigh at least 87 pounds (39.5kg). If her weight fell to 74 pounds (34kg) or less and she refused to gain weight, she would be considered anorexic.

Many anorexics lose even more weight. Most are 20 to 25 percent below the minimum weight recommended for their height. A person who weighs this little will look much too thin. In severe cases, the anorexic might look like a skeleton covered with a layer of skin. Anorexics stay this thin because they are terrified of gaining weight. Robin Lasser writes about her fear of gaining weight, "I kept thinking, 'I'm so hungry. If I let myself eat just one hamburger, I won't be able to stop. I'll eat until I weigh five hundred pounds.' I had to control myself."[4]

People who have anorexia do not think they are too thin. They have a **distorted** view of their own bodies. This means that when they look in the mirror, they do not see wasted, unhealthy bodies. Instead they may see themselves as beautiful and healthy—or they may even feel that they are still too fat. If they gain weight, even a few pounds, they will see themselves as fat even though they are still severely underweight. This distorted view of their bodies is one of the reasons anorexics continue to starve themselves even when they are very thin.

Physical Effects of Anorexia

If a person maintains a low body weight for a long time, some serious health problems can result. Most of these are a direct result of starvation. Because anorexics have no stored fat and do not eat enough food, they may lose muscle tone as their bodies begin to use muscles for fuel. An anorexic's skin may become dry and take on a yellowish tinge. Hair and fingernails may become brittle. Many anorexics feel cold, even when they are in a warm place. This is because they do not have a protective layer of fat to keep them warm. They may grow a layer of soft-downy hair called **lanugo**. Some scientists think the body grows this hair as an attempt to keep itself warm. Many anorexics also suffer from constipation, frequent headaches, dizziness, swelling joints, and sleep disturbances.

Over time, more serious problems can develop. A lack of calcium causes anorexics to lose bone mass. This means that their bones become thin and brittle, and more likely to

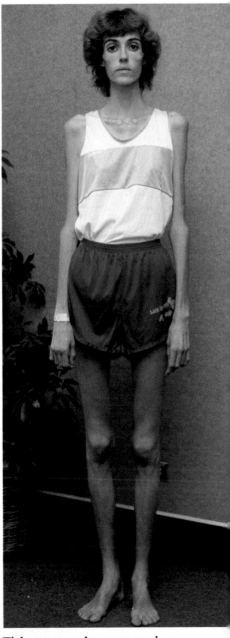

This anorexic woman has reduced herself to skin and bones.

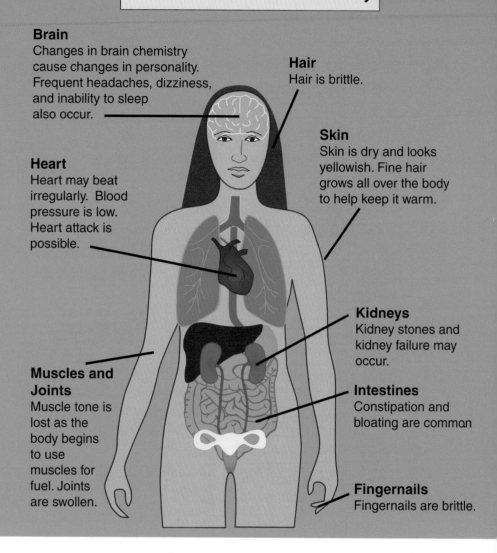

How Anorexia Affects the Body

Brain
Changes in brain chemistry cause changes in personality. Frequent headaches, dizziness, and inability to sleep also occur.

Hair
Hair is brittle.

Skin
Skin is dry and looks yellowish. Fine hair grows all over the body to help keep it warm.

Heart
Heart may beat irregularly. Blood pressure is low. Heart attack is possible.

Kidneys
Kidney stones and kidney failure may occur.

Muscles and Joints
Muscle tone is lost as the body begins to use muscles for fuel. Joints are swollen.

Intestines
Constipation and bloating are common

Fingernails
Fingernails are brittle.

break. In anorexic teenagers, bones may not develop properly. This can result in **osteoporosis**, which persists even if the individual returns to a normal weight. The kidneys, liver, stomach, and intestines can be permanently damaged. The heart can also be affected. An anorexic's heart may beat irregularly. Blood pressure falls and the heart may even shrink in size.

Anorexics are at risk for heart attacks. Anorexia can also affect the brain, literally making it smaller, which can cause changes in personality. In addition, anorexia can halt or delay development during puberty.

Who Gets Anorexia?

Most people who get anorexia are teenage girls or young women. Although boys and men can get anorexia, about 95 percent of anorexics are female. Anorexia often begins when a girl is between sixteen and twenty years old. However, younger children can also get the disorder. Doctors have recently noted an increase of anorexia in eleven- to fourteen-year-olds. They are not sure why, although it may be that dieting is becoming more common in young girls. People over age 25 rarely get anorexia.

It is difficult to know how many people get anorexia because anorexics usually try to hide the disorder. Many anorexics do not get help because they feel ashamed or do not want to admit they have a problem. Health officials believe that about 1 in 100 adolescent girls have anorexia. Ten to 15 percent of the people who develop anorexia will eventually die from it.

Careers and Anorexia

Anorexia is also more common in women who have careers that require them to be thin. Models, dancers, athletes, actors, and other celebrities are at risk for developing anorexia.

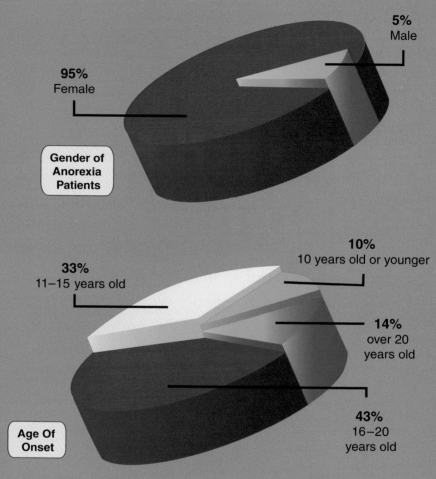

5%
Male

95%
Female

**Gender of
Anorexia
Patients**

10%
10 years old or younger

33%
11–15 years old

14%
over 20
years old

43%
16–20
years old

**Age Of
Onset**

Source: National Association of Anorexia Nervosa and Associated Disorders (ANAD).

Anorexia is most commonly found in the United States and Europe, usually in middle- to upper-class families. The reasons for this, as well as for why anorexia is so common in teenagers and young women, has to do with several factors, including how Western societies view weight and beauty.

Chapter Two

What Causes Anorexia?

Appearance is important to most teenage girls. According to the American Dietetic Association, about 80 percent of teenage girls have tried dieting before they reach age fourteen. Most of these girls will not develop anorexia. To understand why some people develop anorexia while others do not, a variety of factors must be considered. These include the individual's self-image, personality, and brain chemistry. Although every case of anorexia is different, health care professionals have found some common traits that many anorexics share. Social attitudes toward beauty and weight also affect anorexics.

Culture and Anorexia

In Western societies, female beauty is often defined by body size. Thin women are considered beautiful,

Many Western girls idealize the images of thin, young women they see in the media.

while heavier women usually are not. Movies, television, and magazines are full of young, thin women. Even though most healthy women are not as thin as the ones in magazines, many teenage girls and young women see this image as the ideal. As a result, some girls and women feel that their worth as a person is tied to their body size. According to some studies, 80 percent of women are not happy with their bodies. Girls as young as nine years old are dieting, even though they are not overweight.

Anorexics are very focused on their appearance. Starving themselves to attain what they believe is the ideal body gives them the feeling of being admired and valued by society as well as by those around them. Teenagers are especially likely to be influenced by what their friends think. In "Dying to Be Thin," recovered anorexic and former model Kate Dillon talks about how she was teased about her weight when she began junior high:

> They were just horrible to me, telling me I was fat. And whether it was in PE or coming home on the bus every day, they'd stand up, and they would jump up and down and chant, "Overweight Kate. Overweight Kate.". . . I would always wear these massive sweaters . . . and I was sitting in the front seat and just like, trying so hard not to cry, because I was so embarrassed and horrified.[5]

Kate lost 30 pounds (13.6kg) by the end of her seventh-grade year. The importance people place on weight was made clear by the change in the other students' attitude toward her. "Suddenly everyone liked me. My plan worked, sadly and unfortunately. But it seems to be that that's the way the culture is. . . You do what they want and they'll say, 'Cool. Good. You're good now.'"[6]

Self-Image and Anorexia

Most anorexics have a poor **self-image** (sometimes called self-esteem). This means they feel inferior to other people. Rather than feeling confident and sure of herself, an anorexic might feel unworthy and incapable. A person with a poor self-image may try to boost her feelings of self-worth by seeking the approval of others. This is what happened to Andrea, who says, "I was a chubby child growing up with a perfectly skinny twin sister. She seemed to receive all my parents and our peers' attention because she was thin. . . . I thought that going on a diet would increase my self-esteem and get people to notice me."[7]

This negative self-image usually develops during childhood. A child who is criticized, neglected, or ridiculed may grow into a teenager with a poor self-image. Children who are overprotected and forced to obey strict rules are also at risk for developing a poor self-image. Children from this kind of restricted environment do not learn to do things on their own. They do not develop the self-confidence they need to grow into capable adults. Many anorexics report having had difficult childhoods or strained relationships with one or both parents.

Personality and Anorexia

Anorexics are often excellent students and models of good behavior. Most anorexics are **perfectionists**. A perfectionist has an intense need to feel in control. Controlling the amount of food she eats is one way for a perfectionist to achieve this goal. Sometimes a person who feels she does not have much control in her life will strictly limit the amount of food she eats—because it is the only thing in her life she can control. People who live in chaotic environments are also at risk for developing anorexia. By limiting food, these people manage to get at least one aspect of their lives under control.

Perfectionists also set very high standards for themselves. A perfectionist has intense feelings of frustration and guilt if she makes mistakes or fails to meet her own expectations, even if those expectations are impossibly high. By reaching and maintaining a very low weight, the anorexic feels that she is meeting her own high standards.

Some overachievers think that putting on weight is a form of failure.

Anorexic behavior sometimes starts after a traumatic experience, such as the death of a loved one.

People with poor self-images and perfectionist tendencies often have difficulty adjusting to change and stress. Many anorexics can identify a traumatic or stressful time in their lives when they first became anorexic. Among other things, this could be the death of a loved one, divorce of parents, or starting college. Dana's anorexia started when her parents divorced and she and her mother moved to another state. She says, "My life had been changed so drastically, and suddenly I was in a world where the pressures to be thin outweighed most everything else."[8] Some or all of these factors may play a part in causing anorexia. However, recent research has shown that there may be another important factor: biology.

Biology

Eating disorders tend to run in families. This means that a child with a parent who has struggled with an eating disorder has a higher risk of developing an eating disorder. Part of the reason for this may be environmental. A perfectionist parent who is constantly on a diet is likely to model these behaviors to her children. Mary says she learned to diet from her mother: "My anorexia became full blown at 13. I battled food issues for years before that, however.

Some anorexics learn the behavior from a parent who struggles with perfectionism or an eating disorder.

Mom was always on one diet or another, and I often was hooked into becoming her dieting partner."[9]

But some biological factors may also be passed from parent to child. Some scientists believe that a chemical imbalance in the brain may play a role in anorexia. **Serotonin** is a chemical that influences mood and appetite. Anorexics have been found to have high amounts of serotonin in their brains. **Hormones** may also play a role. During puberty, levels of the hormone estrogen increase in a girl's body. High levels of estrogen can cause some girls to avoid eating.

Every case of anorexia is different. The factors that cause anorexia vary from person to person. Different people also cope differently with anorexia. Two traits most anorexics have in common are becoming secretive about how much they eat and developing a wide variety of strategies to avoid eating.

Chapter Three

Living with Anorexia

O nce an anorexic reaches what she considers to be an acceptable weight, she will go to extreme measures to stay at that weight, or even lose more. An anorexic might feel like a failure if she gains even a single pound. She will feel ashamed of her lack of control and will do everything in her power to return to her previous weight.

Staying underweight is not easy. Food is abundant in Western cultures. Aside from regular mealtimes, most people have constant access to food from vending machines, stores, and at parties and other social gatherings. Even though she is always hungry, an anorexic must continue to eat only very small amounts to maintain her low weight. In addition, she may also feel pressure to eat from parents and friends, who might have noticed that she is too thin.

Staying Thin

Anorexics use a variety of strategies to stay thin. Many of these strategies involve ways to avoid eating altogether. Teenagers who still live with their parents often find family mealtimes especially challenging. An anorexic may try to avoid meals by making excuses such as not feeling hungry, having already eaten with friends, or feeling ill or tired. She may schedule activities during mealtimes or simply not show up. If she must sit down with the family, she will take only small portions of food. She may spend most of the meal rearranging the food on her plate rather than eating it. She may take only tiny bites and chew each bite many times before swal-

At mealtimes, many anorexics rearrange the food on their plates instead of eating.

lowing. She may try to hide her food by dropping it into a napkin. She may refuse to eat certain foods, such as meat and desserts. Many anorexics become vegetarians, but they do not eat the wide variety of foods that vegetarians need to stay healthy.

In her diary, Christy described how she avoided eating lunch:

> I've noticed lately that Mom's been putting extra globs of peanut butter on my celery. I think she's trying to trick me into eating more calories, but I'm the one who's tricking her! When I get to school, I throw my lunch away. Then, while my friends scarf down their fat-filled lunches, I spend 30 minutes walking the halls. So not only do I resist consuming calories, I actually burn some! Ha! Who's in charge now?[10]

Another strategy anorexics use to stay thin is compulsive exercise. In *Demystifying Anorexia Nervosa*, Alexander Lucas writes, "One of my patients was so driven to exercise that she monopolized a stair climbing machine at her local Y. She began using it three hours daily, day in and day out, despite her extreme emaciation. The staff at the Y became so concerned that they barred her from using the facility."[11]

It is not uncommon for anorexics to exercise in secret. On top of what looks like normal exercise, such as participating in a sport or working out at a gym, an anorexic may get up early to run a few miles before work or school and do exercises in her room at night. Although her body is weak from lack of food and loss of muscle tone, she will force herself to complete strenuous routines.

Some anorexics use diet pills or **laxatives** to help control their weight. They may also drink alcohol or use prescription or recreational drugs to help deaden their appetites or to keep themselves from constantly thinking about food.

If an anorexic loses control and eats too much, she may force herself to vomit to get rid of it. An individual who does this two or more times a week for more than three months is considered **bulimic**. A person can be both anorexic and bulimic, but most anorexics are not bulimic. This is because most anorexics do not lose control of their eating, so they do not need to force themselves to vomit. An

Many anorexics exercise compulsively as a way to maintain an extremely low weight.

Bulimics force themselves to vomit when they feel they have overeaten.

anorexic may become bulimic if she can no longer stay in strict control of her eating.

Anorexics do not want help from the people around them. When parents and friends show concern about the anorexic's wasted body, she may start to hide her thinness under layers of bulky clothing. She may avoid changing in front of others, wearing a swimsuit, or other situations where people will see how thin she has become. When people try to help her, she will deny there is a problem and insist

Prolonged starvation takes a huge toll on the emotional well-being of anorexics.

that she feels strong and healthy. She may become irritated and irrational. She may throw a temper tantrum, sulk, or withdraw.

Emotional State

As the disorder progresses, the anorexic will experience emotional problems. A person who is constantly hungry is bound to be irritable. Her starving body will lack energy and she will feel weak and tired. In addition, anorexia often causes insomnia. Lack of sleep may affect an individual's mood, energy level, and ability to think clearly and rationally. These factors can make her interactions with family members and friends stressful. She may be more moody and short-tempered. An anorexic may begin to feel misunderstood by the people around her. She may withdraw from activities she used to enjoy, or stop spending time with friends and instead spend most of her time alone. Many anorexics also suffer from depression.

Bizarre eating behavior can be another emotional effect of anorexia. Anorexics often develop strange and complex food rituals. For example, an anorexic may cut her food into a specific number of very small pieces before eating it. She may insist on eating different kinds of food in a specific order or mixing foods in strange

Anorexics often develop bizarre eating rituals such as chewing each bite the same number of times.

ways. She may never allow the fork to touch her lips or may chew each bite exactly the same number of times. These may be indications that the anorexic is also suffering from **obsessive-compulsive disorder**. Lee Hoffman of the National Institute of Mental Health describes the food rituals an anorexic named Deborah developed: "Every day she weighed all the food she would eat on a kitchen scale, cutting solids into minuscule pieces and precisely measuring liquids. She would then put her daily ration in small containers, lining them up in neat rows."[12]

Progression of Anorexia

The longer a person has anorexia, the greater her risk for developing serious and often permanent physical problems. These include stunted growth, kidney damage, and heart problems. An anorexic may also lose the ability to have children. The length of time a person has had anorexia also affects treatment. People who have suffered from anorexia for many years are less likely to make complete recoveries even when they do get treatment.

It is extremely important that people with anorexia get treatment. Anorexics who do not get treatment have a high risk of dying from starvation or from complications from the disorder. About 20 percent of untreated cases of anorexia are fatal. When treated, just 3 percent of cases are fatal. The outlook for recovery is even better when the disorder is treated early.

Chapter Four

Treating Anorexia

Anorexia is usually difficult to treat. One of the biggest challenges is getting the patient to cooperate with the treatment. Because denying the problem is often part of the illness, it is difficult to get an anorexic to admit she needs help. Even if she realizes that she does need help, an anorexic may still resist treatment because she is afraid of losing control and gaining weight.

Another difficulty in treating anorexia is that the patient must be treated for both physical and emotional symptoms. This usually requires a team of several health professionals. This team might include medical doctors, dietary professionals, nurses, occupational therapists, social workers, psychiatrists, and psychologists. Recovery is not an easy road. It can take months or even years for an anorexic to recover completely.

If the disorder is diagnosed early, and if the family of the patient is cooperative, she may be treated at home on an outpatient basis. However, often the anorexia has progressed so far that the patient's life is in danger. In these cases, the patient must be hospitalized.

Hospital Treatment

Once an anorexic is admitted to a clinic, hospital, or treatment center, she will probably stay there for two to six months. If she is extremely weak and underweight, the first part of her stay will involve total bed rest. She will also be put on a **refeeding** program. If she cannot or will not feed herself, she will be fed **intravenously** or with a tube that runs into her throat through her nose. Regaining weight

Treatment for anorexia often begins with a visit to the doctor. Successful treatment, however, usually involves a team of health professionals.

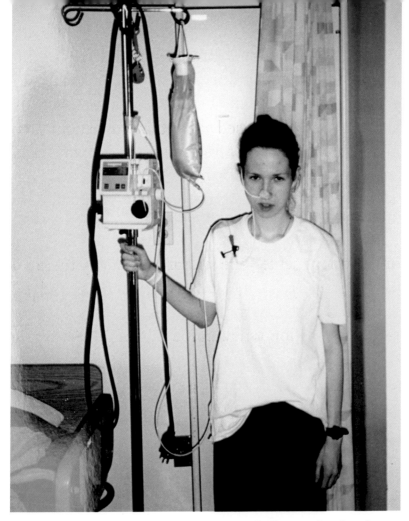

A tube that runs through her nose delivers the food
that this hospitalized anorexic girl needs to gain
weight.

is hard on a weakened and damaged body, so doctors must carefully monitor this first stage of treatment. A gain of a quarter of a pound a day is considered good, safe progress. The next step is to put
the patient on a liquid diet. From there, she can
slowly start eating solid foods.

Once the patient is strong enough to eat on her own and is out of immediate danger, she is put on a strict eating regimen of four to six meals each day. This part of the treatment is usually challenging for the patient. The amount of food she is expected to eat may seem overwhelming to her. Chewing and swallowing that much food may be difficult. She may also have an aversion to many foods—especially those with a high fat or calorie content. Family and hospital support staff may need to help the anorexic learn to eat normally again. Kim, a recovered anorexic, says, "In the beginning one of the biggest challenges is 'gaining weight.' This is so scary! As well as allowing myself to eat, and to eat when I want and what I want. The guilt I felt when eating was phenomenal."[13]

Supervision

Most anorexics must be supervised during mealtimes to be sure they are actually eating. An anorexic who is resisting treatment will do all kinds of things to avoid eating and gaining weight. In *Anatomy of Anorexia,* Steven Levenkron discusses how one anorexic resisted treatment. Anne was five feet, seven inches (169.8cm) tall and dangerously underweight at only 79 (35.8kg) pounds. "Anne had been hiding food under her bed and flushing what she could down the toilet. She was put on a [feeding] tube to prevent her from losing more weight. They found out she had been disconnecting the tube and letting the fluids run into a pitcher, which she would pour down the toilet,"[14] Levenkron writes.

One way to get anorexics to eat is to use rewards and privileges. For example, the patient may be allowed to watch TV or make phone calls only if she eats the required amount of food.

Anorexics who return to a healthy weight before leaving the hospital have the most chance for long-term success. Unfortunately, many anorexics are released too soon, usually because of the high cost of treatment.

Long-Term Treatment

The patient's treatment is not over when she leaves the hospital. Without further treatment she is likely to return to her previous eating habits. Even with treatment, relapses are common. Many anorexics

A nurse in a clinic closely watches an anorexic to make sure that she eats all of her dinner.

return to their old eating patterns and need to be hospitalized again. This cycle can repeat itself several times before the person is finally free of the disorder. In order for treatment to be effective, the patient must explore how and why she became anorexic and learn how to deal with food in a healthy way.

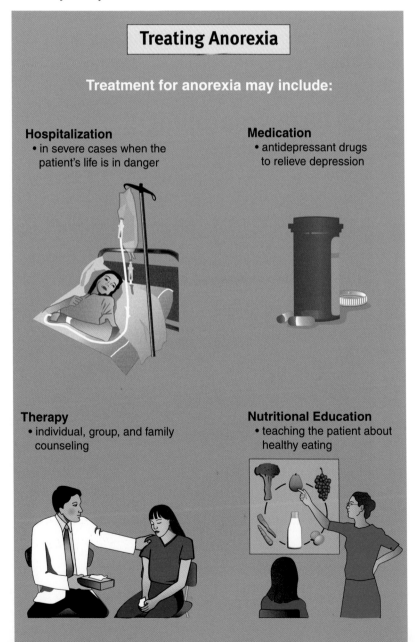

Treating Anorexia

Treatment for anorexia may include:

Hospitalization
- in severe cases when the patient's life is in danger

Medication
- antidepressant drugs to relieve depression

Therapy
- individual, group, and family counseling

Nutritional Education
- teaching the patient about healthy eating

One type of therapy involves teaching the patient about healthy eating and helping her to improve her attitude toward food. The therapist may help the anorexic to choose healthy foods and prepare balanced meals. The anorexic will also learn to exercise appropriately. She may be asked to try new foods or keep a food diary as part of her therapy. The therapist may also help the patient deal with family mealtimes and other social situations where food is present.

Exploring Causes

In order for treatment to be effective, the patient must also explore the causes of her anorexia. This often involves therapy to help with the patient's negative self-image and perfectionist tendencies. Family therapy may be needed to help the patient's family overcome harmful behavior patterns and learn new, more positive ways to relate to each other. Many anorexics also benefit from group therapy. Group therapy gives the anorexic a chance to see aspects of herself in other people with anorexia. This can lead to a greater understanding of her own disorder. Further, group therapy is a place for anorexics to share stories and support one another.

Another method of treatment involves the use of **antidepressant** drugs. These drugs are prescribed by a psychiatrist. Antidepressant drugs do not cure anorexia, but sometimes they can help. Many anorexics are also depressed. The antidepressant drugs help to relieve the symptoms of depression so that the anorexic can focus on her treatment.

Future Outlook

Studies show that 60 percent of anorexics who get treatment make a full recovery. These people do not spend their lives thinking about food. They eat normally, and go on to have families and careers. They consider their battle with anorexia to be an important part of their lives, but one that is in the past.

About 20 percent of treated anorexics make a partial recovery. These people still spend a fair amount of time thinking about weight and food. They diet constantly and have difficulty maintaining meaningful relationships and developing rewarding careers.

The remaining 20 percent struggle with anorexia for their whole lives. They are repeatedly hospitalized and are in and out of treatment. Most cannot maintain friendships or romantic relationships. Holding a job may also be a problem. These patients spend their lives obsessing about food and weight. They may be lonely and depressed. They frequently suffer serious health problems, and some die from the disease.

There is no way to know who will recover from the anorexia and who will not. Even the most severe cases can end happily. Susan is an excellent example of this:

I call my story "success" because that is exactly what it is. I was the definition of an eating disorder. I have been hospitalized more

Anorexics who seek proper treatment have a good chance of making a full recovery.

times than I can count. Most of these hospitals I was dismissed from as "noncompliant" [uncooperative]. My family was told to prepare for my death. I was almost 50% less than my ideal body weight. It has been over a year since my last hospitalization. I am not only alive, but doing well in life. I am in college and for the first time I can remember, I feel happy and healthy.[15]

Knowing what causes anorexia and how to treat it are important steps in the fight against anorexia. Parents, educators, and medical professionals today have a deeper understanding of how the Western obsession with thinness can make girls feel that they are not worthy unless they, too, are thin. One way to fight anorexia is to help girls realize that their self-worth is not tied to their body size.

In addition, people today are more aware of anorexia than they ever have been. This greater awareness has resulted in more anorexics being identified and treated than in past years. Anorexia is not going away anytime soon but people who have anorexia today have a greater chance for recovery than ever before.

Notes

Chapter 1: What Is Anorexia?

1. Eating Disorders, Disordered Culture, "Allie's Story." www.eating.ucdavis.edu/speaking/told/anorexia/allie.html.
2. Christy Heitger-Casbon, "Diary of an Anorexic," *Campus Life,* January/February 2000. www.christianitytoday.com/cl/2000/001/7.50.html.
3. Kim Ratcliffe, e-mail interview with author, February 26, 2005.
4. Eating Disorders, Disordered Culture, "Robin's Story" (Anorexia Nervosa). www.eating.ucdavis.edu/eatdis/anorex/rolan/starve/starve.html.

Chapter 2: What Causes Anorexia?

5. Quoted in PBS, "Dying to Be Thin," transcript, *NOVA,* December 12, 2000. www.pbs.org/wgbh/nova/transcripts/2715thin.html
6. Quoted in PBS, "Dying to Be Thin."
7. Eating Disorders, Disordered Culture, "Andrea's Story." www.eating.ucdavis.edu/speaking/told/anorexia/andrea.html.
8. Quoted in Marlene Boskind-White and William

C. White Jr., *Bulimia/Anorexia: The Binge/Purge Cycle and Self-Starvation.* New York: W. W. Norton, 2000, p. 247.

9. Caringonline, "My Story of Anorexia—Mary." http://caringonline.com/feelings/byvictims/mary .htm.

Chapter 3: Living with Anorexia

10. Heitger-Casbon, "Diary of an Anorexic."
11. Alexander R. Lucas, *Demystifying Anorexia Nervosa: An Optimistic Guide to Understanding and Healing.* New York: Oxford University Press, 2004, p. 86.
12. Lee Hoffman, "Eating Disorders: Anorexia Nervosa," *Selfhelp,* May 28, 1998. www.selfhelp magazine.com/articles/eating/nih/anorexia.html.

Chapter 4: Treating Anorexia

13. Ratcliffe, e-mail interview with author.
14. Steven Levenkron, *Anatomy of Anorexia.* New York: W. W. Norton, 2000, p. 143.
15. Eating Disorders, Disordered Culture, "Susan's Story." www.eating.ucdavis.edu/speaking/told/ anorexia/susan.html.

Glossary

antidepressant: Medication used to treat emotional disorders, including depression, anxiety disorder, and eating disorders.

bulimic: A person who regularly overeats and then forces herself to vomit.

distorted: Not truly or completely representing reality.

hormones: Chemicals that regulate and stimulate cells.

intravenously: Injected into a vein by way of a needle.

lanugo: Soft, downy hair found on a newborn infant or an undernourished person.

laxatives: Medicines that promote bowel movements. Usually used to relieve constipation.

obsess: To think or worry about something constantly.

obsessive-compulsive disorder: A psychological condition characterized by recurrent thoughts and the overwhelming need to perform repetitive, often useless actions.

osteoporosis: A disease that weakens the bones, causing them to break easily.

perfectionists: Persons with very high standards who must get everything right, down to the last detail.

refeeding: The process of gradually returning to a normal diet after starving.

self-image: The opinion a person holds about his or her own worth.

serotonin: A chemical that helps pass messages in the brain and nervous system and that affects emotions.

For Further Exploration

Books

Dan Harmon, *Anorexia Nervosa: Starving for Attention.* Philadelphia, PA: Chelsea House, 1999. This informative book tells about the causes, effects, and treatments for bulimia and anorexia. Includes personal stories from people with the disorders.

Jay McGraw, *The Ultimate Weight Solution for Teens: The 7 keys to Weight Freedom.* New York: Free Press, 2003. This book describes healthy ways for teenagers to lose weight. Addresses both emotional and physical issues. Includes an entire chapter for people with eating disorders.

Paul R. Robbins, *Anorexia and Bulimia.* Springfield, NJ: Enslow, 1998. This book includes a lot of information about these eating disorders. There is also a Q-and-A section and a glossary.

Debbie Stanley, *Understanding Anorexia Nervosa.* New York: Rosen, 1999. This book would be especially helpful to someone who thinks she may have anorexia or who is concerned about someone who has the disorder. There are sections on causes, how to identify the disorder, and how to get help.

Web Sites

ANAD: National Association of Anorexia Nervosa and Associated Disorders (www.anad.org). This is a wonderful site for people who have eating disorders. It offers support, including hotline counseling, referrals, discussions, and information, all free of charge.

ANRED: Anorexia Nervosa and Related Eating Disorders (www.anred.com/welcome.html). This Web site has a wealth of information about anorexia and other eating disorders.

Eating Disorders, Disordered Culture (www.eat ing.ucdavis.edu/default.html). This beautiful and haunting Web site features stories written by people who have suffered with eating disorders, as well as artwork and practical information.

Index

Picture Credits

About the Author

Rachel Lynette has written ten other books for Kid-Haven Press, as well as dozens of articles on children and family life. She also teaches science to children of all ages. Rachel lives in the Seattle area with her two children, David and Lucy; her dog, Jody; and two playful rats. When she is not teaching or writing, she enjoys spending time with her family and friends, traveling, reading, drawing, and in-line skating.